THE FILM BUSINESS 101

A Producer's Guide to Funding,
Production, and Distribution.

MILO SCHWARTZ

Published by:
Milo Schwartz LLC

ISBN: 979-8-9993749-0-5
Library of Congress Control Number: 2025922077

Cover Design by: *Westville Media*
Interior Design & Formatting by: *Westville Media*

Printed in the United States of America.

For more information, visit: *www.filmbusiness101.com*

THE FILM BUSINESS 101: A PRODUCER'S GUIDE TO FUNDING, PRODUCTION AND DISTRIBUTION

DEDICATION

To all the die-hard filmmakers across the globe—

This book is for you.
For the dreamers who turn ideas into reality,
For the storytellers who refuse to quit,
For the creators who see possibilities where others see obstacles,
And for the relentless spirits who believe that one great film can change everything.

Keep pushing, keep creating, and never stop chasing the magic of cinema.

This is your journey.

CONTENTS

Paranormal Activity

Chapter 4:
Episodic vs. Film – Choosing the Right Format
- Self-Contained Films vs. Expanding Narratives
- Funding, Production, and Distribution Differences
- Real Case Studies: Breaking Bad and Stranger Things

Chapter 5:
Distribution & Getting Your Film Seen
- Theatrical Releases vs. Streaming and VOD
- Leveraging Film Festivals to Attract Distributors
- Marketing Strategies: Creating Buzz Before Release

Chapter 6:
Navigating the Business Side of Filmmaking
- Contract Negotiations & Protecting Your IP
- Working with Agents, Managers, and Attorneys
- Real Case Studies: Rocky and Pulp Fiction

MILO
SCHWARTZ

CHAPTER 1:
How the Film Industry REALLY Works (Your First Step to Breaking In)

Imagine this: You're standing outside Paramount Studios in Los Angeles. The famous archway looms over you. You've got a screenplay in your bag, a dream in your heart, and no clue what to do next. How do you turn this into a career? How do you get past those gates—not as a tourist, but as a filmmaker?

Welcome to Hollywood, where ideas are **currency, relationships are everything, and business rules over creativity.**

You're not just here to "break in." You're here to **understand the industry from the inside out**—so that when opportunity knocks, you're ready to answer.

1.1 The First Reality Check: Hollywood is a Business First

Let's set the scene:

You just finished writing your first script. It's brilliant (at least, you think so). You're picturing yourself at the Oscars, accepting Best Director. You call a few production companies, expecting someone to be excited about your masterpiece.

Nobody calls you back.

Why? Because you're thinking like a creative, not a businessperson.

Here's the truth: **Hollywood isn't waiting for you. Investors and studios don't care about your passion— they care about profit.**

A **filmmaker's first job isn't just to create a great film. It's to prove that their film can make money.**

The Industry in One Sentence:
Movies Are Just Really Expensive Products

Think of **film like a business startup.** Would an investor give you $10 million just because you *love* your idea?

No. They invest because they believe your project will make them money.

Your job as a filmmaker isn't just to tell a story. It's to create a film that people want to buy.

The Mistake New Filmmakers Make:
- Thinking a "great idea" is enough to get funding
- Waiting for someone to discover them
- Not understanding how **deals, financing, and distribution** work

The Mindset of a Successful Filmmaker:
-Treats film like a business
- Builds a network before they need it
- Understands how to pitch projects to investors

1.2 Who Actually Runs Hollywood? (The Power Players You Must Know)

You walk into a coffee shop in Los Angeles. The people sitting around you aren't actors—they're **executives, producers, and agents.** These are the people who decide **what movies get made and who gets to make them.**

The Five Most Powerful Players in the Film Business

a. Studio Executives (The Greenlighters)
- They run major studios (Warner Bros, Disney, Netflix, Universal, etc.).
- They control hundreds of millions of dollars and decide which movies get made.

How to Get Noticed by Them:
- Have a **proven track record** (make a short film that wins awards)
- Have a producer or agent **pitch your project**
- Build an audience **before** you approach them (social media, film festivals)

b. Producers (The CEOs of Film)
Producers don't just **make** movies. They **make movies happen.** They are **the real power players** behind Hollywood. Why? Because they **secure financing, hire the team, and make deals.**

If you want to break into the industry, knowing a great producer is more valuable than knowing a director.

How to Get Noticed by a Producer:
- Have a film that's already **gaining traction (festival buzz, social media hype).**
- Be someone who **brings solutions, not just ideas** (ex: "I already have $50K secured").
- Show them how they can **make money from your project.**

Real Story: How Jason Blum Became Hollywood's Most Profitable Producer
Jason Blum (Blumhouse Productions) figured out that **low-budget horror movies make huge returns**.

- Instead of making $100M movies, he made *Paranormal Activity* for **$15,000.**
- It made **$193 million.**
- Now, his company dominates horror (*The Conjuring, Insidious, Get Out*).

Lesson: If you want producers to back your film, show them **how they'll profit from it.** Show them how unique your film is compared to others in the same genre.

c. Sales Agents & Distributors (The People Who Sell Your Film)

Even if you make an incredible film, **you need a distributor to put it in theaters, on Netflix, or on VOD platforms.**

Sales Agents: Act like film brokers. They sell your movie to distributors.

Distributors: Buy films and release them to audiences.

Case Study: How *The Blair Witch Project* Revolutionized Indie Film Distribution

- Made for **$60,000**, sold for **$1.1 million**, made **$250 million**
- **Built a fanbase BEFORE the film was released** (fake documentary, viral marketing)
- Proved that **marketing is just as important as filmmaking**

Lesson: Your film isn't just a product—it's an event. The more buzz you create, the easier it is to sell.

1.3 How Films Get Greenlit (The Only Three Ways to Make a Movie in Hollywood)

It's 9:30 AM at a high-rise office in Beverly Hills. A group of studio executives sits around a long, glass conference table. Stacks of scripts and pitch decks are in front of them. They have one job today: Decide which projects are worth investing in.

One film is greenlit. Another is rejected. Why?

That's what we're going to uncover here. **Who decides what movies get made? What do they look for? And how can you get past the gatekeepers?**

a. Studio Films: The High-Stakes World of Blockbusters

What It Means When a Studio Greenlights a Film
When a studio "greenlights" a film, they are committing **millions (or hundreds of millions) of dollars** to produce, market, and distribute it.

A studio's decision isn't based on passion or creativity— it's based on *risk assessment, brand potential, and market value.*

How Studios Make Greenlight Decisions
If you want to get a studio film made, understand what **execs look for:**

Proven Intellectual Property (IP)
- Studios **love franchises, reboots, sequels, and adaptations.**
- Why? Because **existing IP means built-in audiences and lower risk.**

- *Marvel, DC, Harry Potter, Star Wars—these all guarantee ticket sales.*
- *Even Sonic the Hedgehog got a movie because the IP was valuable.*

A-list Attachments

- If your script has **Leonardo DiCaprio, Margot Robbie, or Tom Cruise attached**, studios are far more likely to invest. (Network strategically to explore opportunities for securing an A-list actor's interest in reading and potentially attaching to your script.).
- **Star power equals marketing power.**

A Bankable Director & Producer

- Directors like **Christopher Nolan, Jordan Peele, or Denis Villeneuve** gets greenlit because they have **a history of delivering hits.**
- **A strong producer backing your film makes studios trust your project.**

A Clear Market Strategy

- Studios don't just greenlight movies—they greenlight **marketing campaigns.**
- A film **must be sellable to a wide audience:**
  - **Who is the target audience?**
  - **How will it be marketed (trailers, viral content, celebrity press)?**

Real Story: How Nolan Got "Inception" Greenlit Christopher Nolan's journey to becoming one of Hollywood's most respected directors didn't happen overnight. Born in London, Nolan developed an early interest in filmmaking, creating short films with his father's Super 8 camera. He later studied English Literature at University College London (UCL), where he used the school's film society equipment to make his early works.

His breakout moment came with *Following* (1998), a low-budget noir thriller shot on weekends over a year using natural light and non-professional actors. The film gained critical acclaim, but it was *Memento* (2000) that put him on Hollywood's radar. This mind-bending indie thriller, told in reverse chronology, earned him an Academy Award nomination for Best Original Screenplay and led to bigger opportunities.

Nolan pitched *Inception* to Warner Bros. in 2002, but they rejected it because:

- It was too risky—a high-budget, original sci-fi movie with no franchise backing.
- Nolan hadn't yet proven himself with big-budget films.

What changed? Instead of giving up, Nolan built his credibility. He took on *Batman Begins* (2005), revitalizing the Batman franchise. With its success, he secured even more studio trust and a larger budget for *The Dark Knight* (2008), which became a billion-dollar blockbuster.

By 2010, Nolan had established himself as a visionary director who could deliver massive box office returns. Warner Bros. finally gave *Inception* the green light with a $160 million budget—because Nolan had now proven he could handle high-stakes, high-budget filmmaking.

Lesson: If you want a studio to take a risk on you, you must first prove you can handle success. Establish credibility, build a strong track record, and create work that showcases your ability to deliver at the highest level.

b. Indie Films: The Art of Making a Movie Without Studio Backing

Indie filmmakers don't have studio funding, but they **still get films made**—by piecing together financing from multiple sources.

How Indie Films Secure Funding

Private Investors – Wealthy individuals who invest for profit (or bragging rights). *(Most have disposable cash)*
Equity Financing – Selling ownership of the film in exchange for funding. *(Giving a percentage of the film)*

Crowdfunding – Kickstarter, Indiegogo, or fan-backed campaigns.

Grants & Tax Incentives – Many governments provide funding for films shot in their region. *(Check your state)*

Pre-Sales – Selling the rights **before filming begins** (especially foreign distribution deals). *(Based on having bankable talent already attached)*

Real Story: How Damien Chazelle Got "Whiplash" Made

- Chazelle wrote *Whiplash* as a feature film but **couldn't get full funding**.
- He **filmed a short version (18 minutes) and submitted it to Sundance**.
- It won the **Short Film Jury Award**, leading to **full funding for the feature.**
- The film made **$49 million worldwide** and won **three Academy Awards**.

Lesson: Sometimes, the best way to get a film made is to **make a short proof-of-concept first.**

c. Self-Financed Films: Making a Movie with Your Own Money

The Reality of Self-Funding:

- If you finance your own movie, **you control everything—but take all the financial risk.**
- Many first-time directors use **personal savings, credit cards, and small investor pools** to fund their first feature.

Real Story: How Robert Rodriguez Made "El Mariachi" for $7,000

- Rodriguez **volunteered for medical experiments** to raise money.
- He shot *El Mariachi* in Mexico using **non-actors and real locations.**
- The film **got into Sundance**, landed a **$1M deal with Columbia Pictures**, and started his career.

Lesson: If nobody is giving you money, **find a way to make your film anyway.**

2. The Hard Truth: Not Every Film Gets Made—Here's Why

Even great scripts and talented directors don't always get greenlit. **Here's why films fail before they start:**

The Budget is Too High for the Concept

- Studios won't fund a **$100M drama about a struggling poet.**
- They would fund a **$100M action film starring The Rock.**
- Solution: **Keep indie budgets LOW to reduce risk.**

✖ The Target Audience is Too Small

- If your film **doesn't appeal to a broad audience**, investors won't fund it.
- Solution: **Clearly define your market and explain how you'll sell the film.**

✖ No Distribution Plan

- Even if you make a film, **without distribution, nobody will see it.**
- Solution: **Secure a distributor or pre-sales agreement before production.**

Chapter 1 Recap: The Film Industry's Reality Check

✓ Hollywood is a business. Money comes first.
✓ If you want funding, show investors how they'll make a profit.
✓ There are only 3 ways to get a film made—Studio,

Indie, or Self-Funded.

✔ Relationships are everything. Build them before you need them.

✔ **Self-Financed Films Require Hustle, Resourcefulness, and Smart Budgeting**

Action Plan: What You Can Do Next

If you have a feature script: Start networking with producers and potential investors.

If you don't have a script yet: Write something **marketable, low-budget, and achievable.**

If you don't have funding: Consider crowdfunding, pre-sales, or making a short proof-of-concept.

Chapter 2:

Developing a Marketable Film Idea (The Blueprint for a Film Investors Will Actually Fund)

Imagine you're sitting in a producer's office. You've spent months refining your screenplay. You're about to pitch it, but before you even finish your first sentence, the producer interrupts:

"Who's your audience? What's the budget? How will this make money?"

If you don't have answers, the meeting is over before it begins.

Having a **great idea isn't enough**—you need to make sure your idea is **marketable, fundable, and commercially viable.**

By the time you finish this chapter, you will:

- Know **how to transform an idea into a fundable project**
- Understand **what investors and distributors look for**
- Be able to **position your film so people WANT to pay for it**

Let's dive in.

1. The Harsh Truth: A Good Idea Isn't Enough

Every filmmaker thinks their idea is great. But **Hollywood doesn't invest in "great ideas"—it invests in profitable ideas.**

Scene 1: The Coffee Shop Reality Check
You're pitching your idea to an investor over coffee. They're nodding politely, but you can tell—they aren't hooked.

You say:
"It's about a struggling poet in 19th-century France who..."

They take a slow sip of coffee. You've lost them.

But what if instead, you said:

"What if there was one day a year where all crime was legal?"

Now they're leaning in. They want to hear more.

Why did one idea fail while the other worked?
- The first was **niche, hard to explain, and had no clear hook.**
- The second was **immediately engaging and easy to visualize.**

Real Story: Why "The Purge" Got Greenlit & Other Films Don't

- *The Purge* was greenlit because it had a **killer one-liner that anyone could understand.**
- The concept was **immediately intriguing**—people could already imagine the movie before seeing it.
- Even if you didn't know the actors or director, **you wanted to see what happened on that one night a year.**

Lesson:
A **strong film concept should instantly grab attention** and make people curious. If you have to explain your idea for **five minutes before someone gets it**, it's too complicated.

How do you fix this?

1. **Refine your core idea.** Can you pitch it in one sentence?
2. **Ask yourself: Would I pay to see this movie?** If you hesitate, rethink your approach.
3. **Test it on friends or colleagues.** If they don't get excited, your pitch isn't strong enough.

2. What Makes a Film Marketable? (Deep Breakdown)

A marketable film isn't just something **you** want to see—it's something **millions of people will want to pay for.**

Imagine you're sitting across from a Hollywood producer. What will convince them to fund your project?

2.1 A High-Concept Idea That Can Be Pitched in One Sentence

Every **marketable** film can be boiled down to a **single, gripping sentence.**
If you can't do this, your idea is **too complicated to sell.**

Strong One-Sentence Pitches:

- *"A washed-up boxer gets a shot at the heavyweight title." (Rocky)*
- *"A man discovers his whole life is a reality show." (The Truman Show)*
- *"A group of criminals try to pull off the perfect heist—but one of them is an undercover cop." (Reservoir Dogs)*

Why This Matters:

- A **one-sentence pitch makes your film easier to sell** to investors, studios, and distributors.
- If your logline isn't strong, **your entire pitch will struggle.**

Personal Exercise: Test Your Logline Right Now

- Imagine you're on **an elevator with Steven Spielberg.**
- You have **10 seconds to pitch your film.**
- What would you say?

Lesson:
If your logline **doesn't spark curiosity, tension, or excitement**, it needs work.
Refine it until it grabs attention immediately.

2.2 A Clear Target Audience (Who Will Pay to Watch It?)

Every successful film has **a specific target audience.**

Nothing is for everyone. If you say, "This film is for
everyone," you're setting yourself up for failure.

Who Your Audience Might Be:

- **Horror Fans:** Love **low-budget, high-thrill**
  experiences (*The Conjuring, Paranormal Activity*).
- **Sci-Fi Fans:** Love **world-building and spectacle**
  (*Blade Runner 2049, Interstellar*).
- **Family Audiences:** Want **fun, wholesome
  entertainment** (*Pixar, Disney movies*).

**Real Story: How "Paranormal Activity" Targeted the
Perfect Audience**

- It wasn't made for the Oscars. It was made for
  horror fans who love viral scares.
- The marketing strategy was **built around social
  media & word-of-mouth buzz.**
- Budget: **$15,000** → Box Office: **$193M**

Lesson:
Your audience must be **specific, defined, and reachable.**
**If you can't describe your audience in one sentence,
your film will struggle to find buyers**

2.3 A Budget That Matches the Concept

An investor doesn't care how creative you are—they care about how they'll get their money back.

If you're making a **$50M indie drama**—that's a problem. If you're making a **$5M action film with strong international appeal**—that's fundable.

Real Story: How Jordan Peele Funded "Get Out"
- Budget: **$4.5M**
- Box Office: **$255M**
- **Why?** It was **cheap to produce** but had a **massive built-in audience.**

Lesson:
Your budget must **match the financial potential of your film.**

Ask Yourself:
- **How much will my film cost?**
- **How much will my audience be willing to spend?**
- **How will I make back the investment?**

If you can't answer these questions, **investors won't take you seriously.**

2.4 A Unique Hook That Separates It from Other Films

The film industry is **crowded**—your idea must have a **fresh angle** that makes it stand out.

Examples of Films With a Unique Hook

- *Bird Box*: A horror movie where the characters **can't use their vision.**
- *A Quiet Place*: A horror movie where the characters **can't make noise.**
- *Knives Out*: A murder mystery that feels **modern, fun, and satirical.**

Real Story: How "District 9" Stood Out in Sci-Fi

- It wasn't a generic alien movie—it was **a documentary-style, politically charged thriller.**
- The **fresh approach** made it stand out and helped it become a hit.

Lesson:

Your film must have **a unique angle that makes it different.**

If your movie feels **too similar to existing films**, investors will pass.

Final Takeaways:
How to Develop a Film That Gets Funded

✓ **Your idea must be high-concept & pitchable in one sentence.**

✓ **Your film needs a clear target audience—nothing is for everyone.**

✓ **Your budget must align with the financial potential of the film.**

✓ **Your movie must have a unique hook that separates it from others.**

Chapter 3:
How to Fund Your Film (The Real Strategy Behind Financing Movies)

You're sitting across from an investor in a glass-walled office in downtown Los Angeles. Your script is solid, your vision is clear—but none of that matters right now. The investor looks at you and asks the only question that really counts:

"How are you going to make me my money back?"

If you don't have a strong answer, the meeting is over before it begins.

Every filmmaker dreams of making movies, but most never do. **Why?** Because they never figure out how to fund their projects.

Filmmaking isn't just an art, it's a **business.** And in business, if you want people to invest in you, you have to prove **you can make them money.**

By the time you finish this chapter, you will:
- Know **the different ways to fund a film—from self-financing to investor-backed models**
- Understand **how to approach investors, pitch them, and close funding deals**
- Learn **how to create a financial plan that makes investors say "yes"**

If you're serious about getting your film made, **this chapter is your blueprint.**

1. The First Reality Check: No One Cares About Your Film Until You Make Them Care

Many filmmakers struggle to get funding because **they think passion is enough.** They believe that if they just tell people how much their film **means to them**, the money will appear.

Here's the truth: Investors don't care about your dreams. They care about **profitability, risk, and return on investment (ROI).**

Personal Exercise: Put Yourself in an Investor's Shoes
Imagine you have **$100,000 to invest in either:**

1. A **risky indie film** with an unproven team, or
2. A **real estate project** that guarantees a return within 12 months.

Which one would you choose?

Lesson:
If you want investors to fund your film, **you must make them feel that their money is safe.**
Your job isn't to **beg for funding**—it's to **present a profitable opportunity.**

2. The Nine Main Ways Films Get Funded

How to Finance Your Film Independently (Creative & Proven Strategies)

Imagine waking up one morning with a decision—you're going to make your film no matter what. No waiting for investors, no hoping a studio magically funds you. You're going to raise the money yourself. But how?

Many of the **most successful filmmakers started out by independently financing their first films.** They didn't wait for permission. **They found creative ways to raise money, stretch their budget, and get the job done.**

Here's exactly **how you can do it too**—with real-world examples.

<u>*There are only 9 real ways to fund a movie.*</u>

2.1 Bootstrapping (Using Your Own Money the Smart Way)

Bootstrapping means **funding your movie using your personal savings, day job income, or credit.**

Case Study: How Kevin Smith Made "Clerks" for $27,575

- He worked at a **convenience store** and shot the film there **after hours** to save on location costs.
- He **maxed out 10 credit cards** (totaling $23K) to pay for equipment and film stock.

- He **cast his real-life friends** to avoid paying actors.
- **Sundance Film Festival changed everything—** Miramax bought the film for **$227,000** and launched his career.

Lesson:

If you have a **low-cost, high-impact idea, investing your own money could pay off.**

- Keep the budget **as low as possible**
- Only use credit if you **have a distribution strategy**
- Be prepared to **do multiple jobs on set yourself**

Your Action Plan:

- Look at your finances—**how much can you realistically contribute?**
- Find ways to **cut your budget down to the essentials.**

2.2 Side Hustling & Stacking Your Budget Over Time

Some filmmakers fund their projects by **building up money over months or years** while working other jobs.

Case Study: How Barry Jenkins Funded His First Short Films

- Worked as a **busboy and warehouse worker** while writing scripts.
- Used his **own money and small grants** to shoot early projects.
- By the time he made *Moonlight*, he already had **industry credibility.**

Lesson:
You **don't need the full budget upfront**—stack money over time while refining your film.

Your Action Plan:

- **Get a side hustle** (editing, cinematography gigs, PA work)
- Save a fixed percentage of your earnings **each month toward your film**

- Look for **film-related work**—you'll build industry relationships **while saving**

2.3 Crowdfunding (How to Get an Audience to Fund Your Movie)

Crowdfunding is **one of the best ways to raise money while building hype for your film.**

Case Study: How Zach Braff Raised $3.1M on Kickstarter for "Wish I Was Here"

- He leveraged **his existing fan base** from *Scrubs*
- Offered **exclusive perks** like set visits, signed posters, and producer credits
- Created a **high-energy pitch video** explaining his vision

Lesson:
Crowdfunding isn't **just about asking for money**—it's about making people **feel invested** in your film.

- Build your audience **before** launching your campaign
- Offer **creative perks** (merch, VIP experiences, producer credits)
- Use **a compelling pitch video** to explain why your film

matters.

Your Action Plan:

- Make a list of **who would support your project right now**
- Plan **a strong crowdfunding campaign with rewards & marketing**
- Start **building an online community before you launch**

2.4 Film Grants (Free Money for Filmmakers!)

There are **hundreds of grants** available for filmmakers—you just have to apply.

Case Study: How Chloé Zhao Used Grants to Fund "The Rider"

- Applied for **Sundance and San Francisco Film Society grants**
- Used grant money to fund production **without taking on debt**
- Film was critically acclaimed, leading to *Nomadland* and an Oscar win

Lesson:

Many filmmakers **skip applying for grants** because they think it's too competitive. But **someone has to win—why not you?**

Your Action Plan:

- Research **film grants in your region**
- Apply to at least **5 grant programs** this month
- Strengthen your application with a **clear artistic vision**

2.5 Sponsorship & Brand Partnerships

Brands are **always looking for ways to get their product in front of audiences.**

If your film aligns with a brand's audience, they **might fund part of your budget.**

Case Study: How "Cast Away" Used FedEx as a Brand Sponsor

- The film prominently featured **FedEx in the story**
- FedEx didn't pay for placement, but they **provided planes, trucks, and branding for free**

- The collaboration **saved the production millions**

Lesson:
If your film has a **natural brand tie-in,** pitch companies
on **sponsorship opportunities.**

Your Action Plan:

- Look at your script—**are there natural brand partnerships?**
- Create a pitch deck explaining **why their brand fits your film**
- Reach out to **local businesses, product companies, and larger brands**

2.6-Investing in Film Equipment & Renting It Out

Instead of raising cash, **some filmmakers invest in gear** that they can use for their film **and rent out to others** to make money.

Case Study: How Indie Filmmakers Leverage Camera Rentals

- Many **buy a RED or Blackmagic camera** and **rent it out to productions** when they aren't using it
- Over time, this allows them to **recoup costs and fund their own projects**

Lesson:

If you're going to spend money on **renting gear for a one-time shoot,** consider **buying and renting it out instead.**

Your Action Plan:

- Research **what equipment is in high demand** in your city
- Invest in **one or two high-value pieces of gear**
- Rent them out to **earn passive income toward your film**

2.7-Private Investors (Convincing People to Bet on Your Film)

Some investors fund films **because they love movies.** Others fund films **because they want a return on investment.**

What Investors Look For:
- A **strong financial plan** (How will they get their money back?)
- A **marketable project** (Will it sell?)
- A **trustworthy team** (Have you done this before?)

Case Study: How Jason Blum Attracts Investors to Low-Budget Horror Films
Blum figured out that horror films could be **cheap to make, but massively profitable.**

- *Paranormal Activity* was made for **$15,000** and earned **$193M.**
- *The Purge* was made for **$3M** and grossed **$89M.**
- Investors **trust Blumhouse projects** because they consistently make money.

Lesson:
If you want investors, **you must show them a proven financial model.**
Your pitch should be **as much about revenue as it is about storytelling.**

Personal Exercise: Build Your Investor Pitch

- **How much money do you need?**
- **What's your sales strategy?**
- **How will investors get their money back?**

2.8-Pre-Sales & Distribution Deals (Selling the Film Before It's Made)

How do pre-sales work?

- You **sell distribution rights in advance** to streamers (Netflix, Amazon) or international buyers.
- These deals **secure funding before filming even starts.**

Case Study: How "Tenet" Was Pre-Sold to Cover a $200M Budget

- Warner Bros. **pre-sold international rights** to recover **80% of costs** before filming.
- This meant the studio **took almost no financial risk.**

Lesson:

If you can secure pre-sales, your film is much easier to fund.

This requires **relationships with distributors and sales agents.**

Personal Exercise: Research Distribution

- What distributors buy **your type of film?**
- How can you **connect with them before production?**

2.9-Film Grants & Tax Incentives (Free Money for Filmmakers)

Governments, film commissions, and non-profits offer **grants and tax incentives** for filmmakers.

Case Study: How "Mad Max: Fury Road" Used Australian Tax Incentives

- The film's budget was **$150M**, but tax rebates covered **over $30M.**
- This made the project much less risky for investors.

Lesson:
Research **what grants and tax breaks are available**—this could make your project more attractive to investors.

Personal Exercise: Find a Film Grant

- Look up **film grants available in your state or country.**

- What's the eligibility? Could you apply?

Chapter 3 Recap: How to Fund Your Film

✓ No one invests in dreams—they invest in profit potential.

✓ **Bootstrapping:** Use savings, work extra jobs, or use credit smartly.

✓ **Side Hustling:** Stack money over time while working industry jobs.

✓ Crowdfunding only works if you build an audience first.

✓ Investors want financial plans, not just passion.

✓ Pre-sales and tax incentives make films less risky for investors.

Next Steps: What You Can Do Right Now

- **Refine your film's financial plan.**
- **Identify at least three funding sources for your project.**
- **Start networking with investors, sales agents, or distributors.**

- If you don't have an audience, start building one now

- When to Wait: The Importance of Securing the Right Amount of Funding

Imagine you're on set, watching your film come to life. But instead of feeling excited, you feel frustrated. The locations aren't what you pictured, the props look cheap, and the VFX budget was slashed so badly that your film is starting to look like an outdated YouTube video.

You wanted to make this movie so badly that you pushed forward before the funding was ready. Now, instead of having a film that could compete in festivals or sell to distributors, you have something that looks rushed, amateur, and unsellable.

This is why **waiting for the right amount of funding** is sometimes the smartest decision a filmmaker can make.

This section will walk you through:
- Real-world examples of films that succeeded because they waited for the right funding
- Examples of films that suffered because they were underfunded
- How to calculate whether you have enough money to

shoot now or need to wait
- What you can do while waiting to raise the rest of
your budget

3.1-The Danger of Underfunding Your Film

Every filmmaker wants to start shooting **as soon as possible.** But here's the hard truth:

A rushed, underfunded film that looks cheap will hurt your career more than not making a film at all.

Real Case Study: The "Fantastic Four" Movie That Was Never Supposed to Exist

- In 1992, **producer Bernd Eichinger** needed to retain the rights to *Fantastic Four*, so he **rushed into production** with a **tiny $1 million budget.**
- The film was **never intended to be released**; it was just made to fulfill a contract.
- The costumes looked cheap, the special effects were embarrassing and the final product was so bad that **Marvel executives bought the film back just to bury it.**

Lesson:

- If your film is underfunded and looks amateurish, **it can kill your reputation.**
- **Sometimes, no film is better than a bad film.**

Your Action Plan:

- Ask yourself: **Would I be proud to show this film to a distributor?**
- If not, **consider waiting to secure more funding** instead of rushing forward.

3.2-When It's Smart to Wait for More Funding

Some films **must** be made at a certain level to work. If your movie relies on **strong VFX, action sequences, or period-specific details**, trying to shoot it on a shoestring budget **could destroy the entire vision.**

Case Study: Why "Mad Max: Fury Road" Took 17 Years to Get Made

- Director **George Miller** wanted to make *Fury Road* in **1998**, but couldn't secure the right budget.
- The film required **expensive desert locations, practical effects, and custom-built vehicles.**
- Instead of compromising, Miller **waited until 2015** when he could get the proper funding ($150M).
- The film won **6 Academy Awards** and made **$375M worldwide.**

Lesson:

- Some films **need a specific budget to work— don't shoot a $50M vision on a $500K budget.**
- **Waiting can result in a masterpiece instead of a disaster.**

Your Action Plan:

- Identify the **bare minimum budget** needed to make your film look professional.
- If you **can't hit that number yet**, develop a strategy to **raise more funding.**

3.3-When It's Smart to Shoot Now (Even on a Low Budget)

Not every movie needs **millions of dollars** to be great. Some of the most successful films were made **on small budgets because they were designed that way.**

Case Study: How "Paranormal Activity" Became a $193M Box Office Smash on a $15K Budget

- *Paranormal Activity* was written **specifically** to be shot cheaply.
- Instead of **expensive VFX**, it used **simple, real-world scares (doors moving, shadows shifting).**
- The result? **A massive profit margin** and a franchise that grossed **nearly $900M.**

Lesson:

- **If your story can be told well on a low budget, don't wait—shoot it now.**
- The key is to **write for the budget you have, not the budget you wish you had.**

Your Action Plan:

- Analyze your script—**could this be rewritten to work on a lower budget?**
- If yes, **shoot now.** If no, **wait and raise the funding you need.**

3.4-How to Calculate Whether You Should Wait or Move Forward

Before deciding whether to **shoot now or wait**, ask yourself:

The Essential Film Budget Questions

1. **Can I make this film look professional with my current budget?**
2. **Will lack of money ruin my film's impact?**
3. **Can I secure more funding within 6-12 months, or will waiting take too long?**
4. **If I wait, will it realistically improve the final product?**

Example Breakdown: Indie Drama vs. Sci-Fi Action Movie

Film Type	Budget Needed for Quality	Can It Be Made on a Small Budget?	Should You Wait for More Funding?
Indie Drama	$50K - $200K	Yes, if locations and actors are strong.	Probably not—can be shot smartly now.
Horror/Thriller	$50K - $500K	Yes, if practical effects are used well.	No, as long as the scares are effective.
Sci-Fi/Action	$500K - $5M+	No, unless you rewrite it to avoid heavy VFX.	Yes, unless you can fund strong visuals.

Your Action Plan:

- Compare your film to **similar successful indie films** and **see what their budgets were.**
- If your film **requires significantly more than what you have**, **consider waiting.**

3.5-What to Do While Waiting for More Funding

Waiting doesn't mean **doing nothing.** There are **productive ways to use this time** so that when funding arrives, **you're 100% ready to roll.**

The Best Uses of Your Time While Raising Funds
- **Strengthen Your Script** – Every great film starts with a rock-solid script.
- **Build an Audience** – Start social media campaigns and build hype.
- **Secure Key Cast & Crew** – Lock in your talent early to make your pitch stronger.
- **Improve Your Pitch Deck** – Investors love **well-prepared filmmakers.**
- **Develop Relationships with Distributors** – The more demand for your film, the easier it is to get funding.

Case Study: How "Moonlight" Used Extra Time to Refine Everything

- Director **Barry Jenkins** spent years perfecting *Moonlight* while waiting for the right funding.

- Instead of rushing into production, he **built industry connections** and **honed his artistic vision.**
- The result? The film **won Best Picture at the Academy Awards.**

Lesson:
Waiting isn't wasted time if you use it wisely.
The **better prepared you are**, the easier it is to secure investors.

Your Action Plan:

- Make a **list of everything you can improve while waiting.**
- Focus on **building relationships, refining your pitch, and expanding your network.**

Final Recap: When to Wait and When to Shoot

✓ **If your budget is too low to do your vision justice, wait and raise more.**
✓ **If your film can be shot smartly with a lower budget, go for it.**

✓ Use your waiting time to refine your script, build your audience, and strengthen your pitch.

✓ Rushing into production with no money can kill your career—be strategic.

Next Steps: What You Can Do Today

- Evaluate your film's current funding—do you have enough to make it look professional?
- If you need more money, build a 6-12 month plan to secure it.
- If waiting, create a list of ways to strengthen your film while raising funds.

Chapter 4:

Episodic vs. Film:

Which One is Right for Your Project?

You have a compelling story. But should it be a movie or a TV series?

Do you go the traditional film route—self-contained, festival-ready, with a clear beginning, middle, and end? Or do you stretch your narrative across multiple episodes, building characters over time and capturing an engaged audience week after week?

Making this decision is critical, because films and episodic content (TV series, streaming series, web series) have completely different funding models, distribution strategies, and audience expectations.

By the time you finish this section, you will:

- Understand the key differences between making a film vs. a TV series.

- Learn how funding, production, and distribution change based on format.

- Be able to decide which format is best for your project.

1. The Core Difference: Self-Contained Story vs. Expanding Narrative

The fundamental difference between film and episodic storytelling is **how the story is structured and consumed.**

Films

- **One self-contained story** (90–180 minutes long).
- **Designed for a single experience** (theatrical, streaming, or VOD).
- **More expensive upfront**, but **lower long-term financial risk.**

Episodic (TV or Streaming Series)

- **A story told in multiple parts (episodes).**

- **Designed for continuous engagement** (weekly or binge-watched).
- **Lower upfront cost per episode**, but **requires long-term commitment.**

Key Takeaway:

- If your story **has a clear, powerful conclusion**, a film might be the best fit.
- If your story **is character-driven, expandable, or has cliffhangers**, episodic might be better.

Your Action Plan:

- Break down your story **into key moments**—does it work better in a single sitting or across multiple chapters?

2. Funding Differences: Who Pays for Films vs. TV Shows?

Funding is **very different** depending on whether you're making a movie or a series.

How Films Are Funded

- **Investors & Production Companies** (They invest in films with strong market potential).
- **Grants & Film Commissions** (Many regions offer incentives for indie films).
- **Crowdfunding & Private Investors** (Popular for indie features).
- **Pre-Sales & Distribution Advances** (Selling rights before filming starts).

How Episodic Projects Are Funded

- **Networks & Streaming Platforms** (Netflix, HBO, Hulu, Amazon fund original series).
- **Pilot-to-Series Model** (Make a pilot, pitch it, and hope for a full season order).
- **Private Investors & Co-Production Deals** (Common in the streaming era).
- **Ad Revenue & Sponsorships** (Web series often rely on brand deals).

Real Case Study: How "Paranormal Activity" Got Funded as a Film Instead of a Series

- The concept **could have worked as a series** but was **packaged as a found-footage horror film.**
- The production budget was **only $15,000**, but **because it was a film, it was easier to sell to theaters.**
- The result? A **$193M box office return** and a franchise.

Lesson:

- **Films require one-time funding but need strong upfront investment.**
- **TV requires ongoing funding, which means you need buy-in from a network or streamer.**

Your Action Plan:

- If **you can secure a full-season commitment, episodic is a great choice.**
- If **you have a smaller budget but a clear marketable concept, a film might be safer.**

3. Production: How Shooting a Movie is Different from a TV Series

Filmmaking and TV production have **vastly different workflows, crew requirements, and schedules.**

Film Production

- **Shot as a single, continuous project** (filming in a few months).
- **Big-budget films require elaborate production schedules.**

- **Post-production is longer, with time dedicated to editing, VFX, and marketing.**

Episodic Production

- **Shot episode-by-episode (or block shooting multiple episodes).**
- **Different directors may direct different episodes.**
- **Faster turnaround times for post-production.**

Real Case Study: How "Breaking Bad" Was Almost a Film

- Vince Gilligan originally pitched *Breaking Bad* as a **movie.**
- But he realized **Walter White's transformation couldn't be rushed**—a TV series gave him the space to tell the full story.
- It became **one of the most successful and critically acclaimed TV shows ever.**

Lesson:

- **If your story relies on long-term character development, episodic storytelling is better.**
- **If your story is tightly contained and doesn't need expansion, film is the right format.**

Your Action Plan:

- Ask yourself: **Will my story suffer if I have to tell it in one sitting?** If yes, consider episodic.

4. Distribution: How Your Project Gets Seen in Each Format

Once your film or series is complete, **how it reaches an audience varies dramatically.**

How Films Are Distributed

- **Film Festivals** (Sundance, Cannes, TIFF).
- **Theatrical Releases** (If backed by a studio or distributor).
- **Streaming Platforms** (Netflix, Hulu, Amazon, Apple).
- **VOD Sales & Rentals** (iTunes, Google Play, YouTube).

How TV Series Are Distributed

- **Network & Cable TV** (HBO, ABC, NBC, CBS).
- **Streaming Platforms** (Netflix, Hulu, Disney+).

- **Web Series & Digital Distribution** (YouTube, Patreon, Vimeo).

Real Case Study: Why "Stranger Things" Was a Series Instead of a Film

- The Duffer Brothers originally **pitched Stranger Things as a movie.**
- Networks rejected it **because the story was too rich for a single film.**
- Netflix greenlit it as an **episodic series, leading to one of the biggest hits in streaming history.**

Lesson:

- **If your story is a binge-worthy concept, consider making it a series.**
- **If your story is contained and has festival potential, film might be a better bet.**

Your Action Plan:

- Research **where your audience watches content**—that will help determine which format to pursue.

5. Long-Term Revenue Potential: Which Format Makes More Money?

Money matters in filmmaking. But how do **films and TV series make money differently?**

How Films Make Money

- **Box Office Sales** (Theater tickets).
- **Streaming Licensing** (Selling rights to Netflix, Amazon, etc.).
- **VOD Sales & Rentals.**
- **Merchandising & Brand Deals.**

How TV Series Make Money

- **Network Deals & Syndication** (Re-airing episodes on different networks).
- **Subscription Revenue** (Netflix & Hulu originals).
- **Ad Revenue (if on TV or YouTube).**

Real Case Study: How "The Office" Made Over $500M from Syndication

- The Office's **long-term revenue didn't come from initial TV ratings**—it came from **streaming and syndication deals**.

- Even years after ending, it's still generating **millions annually** from reruns.

Lesson:

- **TV has long-term money-making potential, but only if it's successful.**
- **Films make money upfront, but their revenue stream can dry up faster.**

Your Action Plan:

- If you **want a long-term passive income stream, episodic might be the smarter choice.**
- If you **prefer big upfront paydays, film is a better bet.**

Final Recap: Should You Make a Film or a TV Series?

✓ **Choose a Film if:** You have a self-contained story that works best in one sitting.

✓ **Choose Episodic if:** Your story benefits from character growth and long-term engagement.

✓ **Consider Funding:** TV requires ongoing financing,

while films need a strong upfront investment.

✓ **Look at Distribution:** TV series thrive in streaming, while films often start in festivals.

Next Steps: Take Action Today

- Analyze your story—does it work better as a movie or a series?
- Research distribution options for both formats.
- Plan your funding strategy based on which format you choose.

Chapter 5:

Distribution & Getting Your Film Seen

You've spent months—maybe years—bringing your film to life. The shoot is wrapped, the editing is done, and now you're staring at the final cut. But here's the reality: A great film sitting on a hard drive does nothing for your career. Now comes the most crucial phase—getting your film seen by the right audience, distributors, and platforms that will turn it into a success.

Distribution is where many filmmakers fail. They focus so much on production that they forget to plan how their film will actually reach viewers. Without a **strong distribution and marketing strategy**, your film will get lost in the endless ocean of content.

By the end of this chapter, you will learn:

- **How film distribution works in today's industry**
- **The different types of releases: theatrical, streaming, and VOD**
- **How to submit your film to festivals and attract buyers**
- **How to create buzz and market your film effectively**

This is the final and most important stage—because if no one sees your film, all your hard work was for nothing.

1. Understanding Film Distribution: The Path from Final Cut to Audience

Let's set the scene.
You've just finished your indie film. Now, you're wondering:
1. Do I submit it to festivals?
2. Should I approach a distributor directly?
3. Can I sell it to Netflix, Amazon, or HBO?
4. Should I self-distribute on VOD platforms like iTunes or YouTube?

Each of these **is a different distribution path** and choosing the right one can **make or break your film's success.**

The Three Main Distribution Paths:

1. **Traditional Theatrical Release** (Big screens, major distributors)
2. **Streaming & VOD (Video-On-Demand)** (Netflix, Amazon, iTunes, etc.)
3. **Festival Circuit & Sales Agents** (Selling your film to the highest bidder)

Each path has advantages and challenges, which we'll break down next.

2. The Traditional Theatrical Release: What It Takes to Get on the Big Screen

For many filmmakers, **seeing their movie in theaters is the dream.** But theatrical distribution is **hard to secure and expensive to execute.**

How Theatrical Distribution Works

1. A distributor **buys the rights** to your film.
2. They plan a **release strategy** (regional, national, or global).

3. They handle **marketing, promotion, and theater negotiations.**
4. The film is shown in **cinemas, drive-ins, or specialty screenings.**

Real Case Study: How "Everything Everywhere All At Once" Succeeded in Theaters

- A24 took a **low-budget, indie sci-fi movie** and turned it into an **award-winning global hit.**
- They used **targeted marketing** to build hype in niche communities.
- The film grossed **over $140M worldwide**, proving **theatrical still works if done right.**

Lesson:

- Theatrical **only works if you have strong marketing and a distributor backing you.**
- If you don't have a major studio deal, **a limited theatrical release or special event screenings might be smarter.**

Your Action Plan:

- If you want a theatrical release, start talking to **sales agents and indie distributors** now.

3. Streaming & VOD: The Most Powerful Modern Distribution Method

Streaming is now the dominant way people watch films.
Netflix, Amazon, Hulu, Apple, and HBO Max **are constantly acquiring films**, but getting on these platforms isn't as simple as uploading your movie.

How Streaming & VOD Distribution Works:

- **You license your film** to a streaming platform.
- The platform **pays upfront or shares revenue** based on views.
- Some deals are **exclusive** (Netflix buys full rights) or **non-exclusive** (your film can be on multiple platforms).

Real Case Study: How "Roma" Became Netflix's First Prestige Film

- *Roma* (Alfonso Cuarón's film) was released **on Netflix instead of theaters.**
- The film gained **massive viewership worldwide**, something it **wouldn't have achieved in limited theaters.**
- It won **Best Picture at the Academy Awards, proving that streaming films can be prestigious.**

Lesson:

- Streaming can **give indie films global exposure without the costs of theatrical.**
- **Netflix and Amazon don't accept blind submissions**—you need an agent or sales rep.

Your Action Plan:

- Research **distribution platforms** that fit your film's genre and audience.
- If aiming for Netflix, **network with acquisition reps and sales agents.**

4. Film Festivals & Sales Agents: Selling Your Film to Distributors

Why Film Festivals Matter

Film festivals **are the best way for indie filmmakers to get noticed by buyers, distributors and industry professionals.**

Major Film Festivals That Attract Distributors:
Sundance – The best festival for indie films and major distributor deals.
Toronto International Film Festival (TIFF) – Where Oscar contenders and indie gems are bought.
Cannes Film Festival – The premier European festival for international distribution.
SXSW (South by Southwest) – Great for genre films, comedies, and unique indie projects.

Real Case Study: How "Whiplash" Started as a Short & Became an Oscar-Winning Film

- Damien Chazelle's *Whiplash* started as a **short film at Sundance.**
- After winning awards, he got **funding for a full feature.**
- The full-length film **debuted at Sundance, was bought by Sony, and won 3 Academy Awards.**

Lesson:

- Festivals can **turn a no-budget indie film into a major success.**

- **Winning at Sundance, TIFF, or SXSW almost guarantees a distribution deal.**

Your Action Plan:

- If your film is festival-worthy, **start applying early.**
- Research **which festivals fit your film's style and audience.**

5. Marketing Your Film: Creating Demand Before Release

Even if you secure distribution, **marketing is crucial.**

Essential Film Marketing Strategies:

☑ **Trailers & Posters** – Your film needs a **professional-looking teaser** to generate interest.

☑ **Social Media Strategy** – Build an audience **months before release.**

☑ **Film Reviews & Press** – Get coverage from movie blogs, YouTube reviewers, and critics.

☑ **Early Screenings & Word of Mouth** – Let influencers and tastemakers watch first.

Real Case Study: How "The Blair Witch Project" Used Guerrilla Marketing to Make $250M

- Before release, the filmmakers **created fake missing-person reports** online, making audiences think the story was real.
- They **built hype on early internet forums and college screenings.**
- The result? **A $250M box office return on a $60K budget.**

Lesson:

- Marketing **matters just as much as making a great film.**
- **The more buzz you generate before release, the more people will watch.**

Your Action Plan:

- Develop a **marketing plan 3–6 months before release.**
- **Leverage social media, trailers, and influencer marketing.**

Final Recap: How to Get

Your Film Seen & Sold

✔ Theatrical releases require strong distributor backing and marketing.

✔ Streaming & VOD give filmmakers global exposure.

✔ Film festivals & sales agents can help sell your film to distributors.

✔ Marketing is essential—hype matters before release.

Next Steps: Take Action Today

☑ Decide which distribution path fits your film best.

☑ If aiming for festivals, research deadlines & submission requirements.

☑ Start building a marketing plan NOW.

Working with an Aggregator: The Key to Getting Your Film on Major

Platforms

You've finished your film, and now you want it on major streaming and VOD platforms like Netflix, Amazon, iTunes, or Google Play. But there's a problem—these platforms don't accept direct submissions from filmmakers.

This is where an aggregator comes in.

5.1-What is an Aggregator, and Why Do You Need One?

An **aggregator is a company that acts as a middleman between filmmakers and digital platforms** like Apple TV, Amazon Prime, Google Play, Vudu, and sometimes even Netflix and Hulu.

What Aggregators Do:
☑ **Submit Your Film to Digital Platforms** – They handle the technical requirements and ensure your film is accepted.
☑ **Handle Quality Control (QC)** – Platforms like iTunes have strict quality standards; aggregators make sure your film meets them.
☑ **Optimize Metadata & SEO** – They ensure your film

appears correctly in searches.

☑ **Help with Pricing & Release Strategy** – Some aggregators offer guidance on how to price your film for rental or purchase.

Key Takeaway:

Without an aggregator, **you cannot directly get your film onto iTunes, Google Play, or other major TVOD (Transactional Video-On-Demand) platforms.**

Your Action Plan:

- Research reputable **aggregators** that specialize in indie film distribution.
- Compare their fees and services **before signing any agreements.**

5.2-How to Choose the Right Aggregator for Your Film

Not all aggregators are the same—some **charge upfront fees**, while others take a **percentage of sales**.

Popular Aggregators for Indie Filmmakers:

☑ **FilmHub** – No upfront fees, but they take a revenue

share.

☑ **Bitmax** – Charges an upfront fee but gets films onto multiple platforms.

☑ **Quiver Digital** – Specializes in iTunes, Google Play, and Amazon submissions.

☑ **Distribber (No Longer in Business)** – Was a popular option, but shut down due to financial issues (a cautionary tale for filmmakers).

How to Choose the Best One:

- If you **don't want to pay upfront**, go with an aggregator like **FilmHub** that takes a revenue cut. (Still take a look at their reviews)
- If you **want 100% of your revenue**, go with an **upfront-fee aggregator** like **Bitmax.** (Still take a look at their reviews)

Real Case Study: How a Filmmaker Used an Aggregator to Get on iTunes & Amazon

- An indie filmmaker made a horror film with **a $50K budget.**
- Instead of trying to get a distributor, he **used an aggregator to self-distribute on Amazon, iTunes, and Google Play.**
- He marketed the film himself and **earned over $250K in digital sales.**

Lesson:

- **Aggregators give indie filmmakers control over their release.**
- If a distributor won't pick up your film, **self-distribution through an aggregator is a great option.**

Your Action Plan:

- Contact at least **two aggregators** and ask about their pricing, platform reach, and contract terms.

5.3-The Costs & Revenue Model of Using an Aggregator

Using an aggregator **is not free.** You need to factor in **costs vs. revenue potential.**

Typical Aggregator Fees:

- **Upfront Fee Model:** $1,000–$3,000 per platform submission.
- **Revenue Share Model:** 20–30% of your earnings go to the aggregator.

How Much Money Can You Make?

- iTunes rentals **range from $3.99–$5.99 per view.**
- Google Play purchases **range from $9.99–$14.99 per film.**
- Amazon Prime pays **based on hours streamed (for Prime Video Direct releases).**

Example: Revenue Breakdown for a Self-Distributed Indie Film

Platform	Price Per Sale	Units Sold	Total Revenue	Aggregator Fee (30%)	Filmmaker's Earnings
iTunes	$9.99	10,000	$99,900	-$29,970	$69,930
Google Play	$12.99	5,000	$64,950	-$19,485	$45,465
Amazon Prime	Pay-per-stream	100,000 hours watched	$50,000	-$15,000	$35,000

Lesson:

- **If your film has strong marketing, aggregators can help you make real money.**
- **Upfront-fee aggregators make sense if you expect high sales volume.**

Your Action Plan:

- If you're **confident in your marketing strategy**, go for a **fee-based aggregator** to keep 100% of revenue.
- If you **want less risk**, go with a **revenue-sharing model.**

5.4-When to Use an Aggregator vs. When to Get a Sales Agent

Use an Aggregator If:

✔ You want **control over your film's release.**

✔ You have a **strong marketing strategy** and can drive traffic yourself.

✔ No distributors have picked up your film, but you **still want a professional release.**

Use a Sales Agent If:

✓ You want **a distributor to handle negotiations and placement.**

✓ Your film has **festival buzz and can attract buyers.**

✓ You want to target **theatrical or larger streaming deals.**

Real Case Study: How "Tangerine" Used Both an Aggregator & a Sales Agent

- The indie film *Tangerine* was shot on **an iPhone for $100K.**
- It played at **Sundance and got buzz, but no major studio deal.**
- The filmmakers used **a sales agent to sell rights to Magnolia Pictures.**
- Magnolia **used an aggregator to get the film on iTunes & Amazon.**

Lesson:

- **Sales agents help if you have a festival hit, but aggregators allow you to go direct.**
- **Sometimes, combining both strategies is the best move.**

Your Action Plan:

- If your film **doesn't attract a distributor, go the aggregator route.**
- If your film is **getting strong festival interest, seek out a sales agent.**

Final Recap: How to Use an Aggregator for Film Distribution

✓ Aggregators help filmmakers get on iTunes, Google Play, Amazon, and VOD platforms.

✓ They handle the technical process, metadata, and quality control for submissions.

✓ Some charge upfront fees, while others take a percentage of sales.

✓ Self-distribution via aggregators is a smart alternative if no distributor picks up your film.

✓ If your film has strong marketing, aggregators can help you generate real revenue.

Next Steps: Take Action Today

☑ Research at least two aggregators and compare their pricing and services.

☑ Decide if you want to pay upfront or use a revenue-sharing model.

☑ If using an aggregator, build a marketing plan to drive traffic to your film.

Chapter 6:
Navigating the Business Side of Filmmaking

Filmmaking is not just about creativity—it's about securing deals, protecting your work, and understanding the legal and financial aspects of the industry. Many great filmmakers struggle because they don't grasp the business side of film. This chapter ensures you avoid costly mistakes and learn how to protect your career.

By the time you finish this chapter, you will:
☑ **Understand film financing structures and revenue-sharing models**
☑ **Know how to negotiate contracts and protect your creative rights**
☑ **Learn when to work with agents, managers, and attorneys**

✅ **Gain insights into networking and building industry relationships**

This chapter will help you **avoid bad deals, maximize your earnings, and set yourself up for long-term success in the industry.**

1. Contract Negotiations & Legal Protection

Why Contracts Matter in Filmmaking

In Hollywood (and even indie filmmaking), a bad contract can destroy your career.

- If you don't protect your rights, **someone else can profit from your work.**
- If you don't negotiate properly, **you could lose creative control of your film.**
- Every film deal, from actor agreements to distribution rights, should be legally documented.
- **Verbal agreements mean nothing in Hollywood**—always have written contracts.

Real Case Study: The "Coming to America" Lawsuit

- A writer, Art Buchwald, sued Paramount, claiming they used his idea without credit.

- Because he had documentation, he **won the lawsuit and received compensation.**

Lesson:

- **Always have contracts reviewed by an entertainment lawyer.**
- **Even small indie films should have signed agreements between crew and cast.**

Your Action Plan:

- Hire or consult with an **entertainment attorney** before signing contracts.
- **Register agreements** with the Writers Guild of America (WGA) if applicable.

Real Case Study: How Sylvester Stallone Protected His Creative Control Over "Rocky"

- Stallone wrote *Rocky* and had multiple studios interested.
- The studios **wanted to buy the script—but wouldn't let him star in it.**
- He refused to sell unless he played the lead role, **even though he was broke.**
- Eventually, United Artists agreed, and *Rocky* became a **$225M blockbuster.**

Lesson:

- **If you don't fight for your creative vision, someone else will change it.**
- **Know when to walk away from a bad deal, even if you need the money.**

Your Action Plan:

- **Read every contract carefully**—if you don't understand it, get a lawyer.
- **Negotiate creative control**—don't give up your vision for a paycheck.

2. Working with Agents, Managers, and Attorneys

Understanding Representation

- **Agents** secure jobs and negotiate deals.
- **Managers** develop your career and provide strategic guidance.
- **Attorneys** handle contracts, IP protection, and legal disputes.

Pros & Cons of Representation

 **Pros:**

- Agents help you get high-profile deals.
- Managers guide long-term career growth.
- Lawyers protect you from predatory contracts.

✕ Cons:

- Agents take 10% of your earnings.
- Managers typically take 15% and aren't always necessary.
- Some attorneys charge hefty upfront fees.

The Difference Between Agents, Managers & Attorneys

Role	What They Do	When You Need One
Agent	Gets you jobs, negotiates contracts, finds deals	When you start getting major industry attention
Manager	Helps shape your career, advises on long-term	When you need career guidance & networking

Role	What They Do	When You Need One
	strategy	support
Attorney	Handles legal contracts, protects your rights	Any time you sign a deal or need legal protection

Real Case Study: How Quentin Tarantino's Attorney Helped Him Get Final Cut on "Pulp Fiction"

- Tarantino's **contract for *Pulp Fiction* originally gave the studio editing control.**
- His **entertainment lawyer renegotiated the deal**, ensuring Tarantino got **final cut approval.**
- This allowed Tarantino to **keep his vision intact**, leading to one of the most iconic films ever made.

Lesson:

- **Entertainment lawyers are just as important as agents & managers.**
- **Never sign a contract without a legal review— small clauses can change everything.**

Your Action Plan:

- If you **start getting big offers**, hire an **entertainment lawyer first.**

- When you **have multiple projects lined up**, consider **an agent or manager.**

Your Action Plan:

- **Don't rush into signing with an agent or manager**—wait until you have momentum.
- Consult an **entertainment attorney** before signing any deal.
- **Research reputable agencies** like CAA, WME, and UTA.

3. Protecting Your Intellectual Property (IP): How to Keep Your Film & Ideas Safe

You've written a killer script. You've developed a brilliant pitch deck. You're excited to share your idea with investors, studios, or potential collaborators. But here's the danger—if you haven't protected your work, you're leaving yourself open to theft.

The film industry is filled with stories of creators who had their ideas stolen because they didn't take the right legal precautions. Don't let that happen to you.

By the time you finish this section, you will:

✅ **Understand how to properly register and copyright your work**

✅ **Know how to protect your pitch decks, treatments, and scripts before sharing them**

✅ **Learn from real cases where filmmakers lost their IP due to poor protection**

If you do **nothing else**, make sure you **protect your creative work before showing it to anyone.**

3.1-The First Rule: Never Share Your Work Without Legal Protection

Why You Must Protect Your Work Before Pitching It

- Hollywood is **notorious for IP theft**—just because someone hears your idea doesn't mean they won't claim it as their own.
- **Verbal agreements mean nothing**—if it's not legally documented, you have no proof you created it first.
- **Even industry professionals** may "borrow" your ideas if they see value in them.

Real Case Study: The "Gravity" Lawsuit

- In 2013, the film *Gravity* (starring Sandra Bullock) became a massive hit.
- A writer named Tess Gerritsen claimed that **Warner Bros. used elements from her novel without permission.**
- Because she didn't have the proper legal protections in place, **her lawsuit was dismissed.**

Lesson:

- **If you don't register your work, you have no legal standing in court.**
- **Hollywood operates on contracts, not trust— never assume people will "do the right thing."**

Your Action Plan:

- Before you **pitch, share, or send out your script or deck**, take the **following legal steps** to protect your IP.

3.2-How to Legally Protect Your Screenplay & Film Concepts

Step 1: Register Your Script with the Writers Guild of America (WGA)

☑ The **WGA registration** proves **you created your script or pitch first**.

☑ It acts as **legal evidence** in case of a dispute.

☑ It costs only **$20 (WGA West) or $10 (WGA East) and lasts for five years**.

Step 2: File for Copyright Protection

☑ Registering your script with **the U.S. Copyright Office** gives you **stronger legal protection**.

☑ This ensures **no one can profit off your work without your consent**.

☑ **Cost:** $45–$65 per registration.

Real Case Study: The "Coming to America" Lawsuit

- Writer Art Buchwald **claimed that Paramount stole his original idea** for *Coming to America* (1988).
- Because he had **registered his concept, he was able to sue and win a settlement**.
- Paramount **tried to claim they came up with the idea first**, but **Buchwald's registration proved otherwise**.

Lesson:

- **WGA registration is helpful, but copyright is the strongest legal protection.**
- **If a major studio steals your idea, you need legal proof that you created it first.**

Your Action Plan:

- **Register your screenplay with the WGA** (quick and easy).
- **For full protection, file a copyright** with the U.S. Copyright Office.

3.3-Protecting Your Pitch Decks, Treatments & Unfinished Concepts

How to Prevent Someone from Stealing Your Pitch

- If you're pitching a TV show or film concept, **you may not have a full script yet.**
- Studios, producers, or executives might **hear your idea and develop a "similar" project later.**
- **This happens often in Hollywood.**

Example: The "Stranger Things" Lawsuit

- In 2018, filmmaker Charlie Kessler sued the **Duffer Brothers, claiming they stole his idea** for *Stranger Things*.
- Kessler had **pitched them a similar concept years earlier but had no legal agreement in place.**
- The lawsuit was **settled out of court**, but it's an example of what happens **when IP isn't properly protected.**

Lesson:

- **If you pitch an idea without legal protection, you may lose it.**

Your Action Plan:
☑ **Before pitching, get a Non-Disclosure Agreement (NDA)** signed.
☑ **Register pitch decks & treatments with WGA** for extra security.
☑ **If possible, copyright your concept (if it's developed enough).**

3.4-The Cost of Cutting Corners: What Happens If You Don't Protect Your IP?

Real Case Study: How "The Matrix" Faced Multiple IP Lawsuits

- *The Matrix* (1999) was **accused of stealing ideas from multiple sources.**
- **Sophia Stewart claimed** that elements were lifted from her unpublished book, *The Third Eye.*
- **Another writer, Thomas Althouse, also sued**, claiming similarities to his script *The Immortals.*
- The lawsuits **dragged on for years**, costing **millions in legal fees.**

Lesson:

- If you **don't register your work**, you may not be able to prove it was stolen.
- If you **try to sue later**, the cost of legal fees could be more than you can afford.

Your Action Plan:

☑ Take legal steps upfront—before sharing your work.

☑ If you suspect someone is copying your idea, consult an entertainment lawyer immediately.

3.5-How to Take Legal Action If Your Work is Stolen

If someone **takes your idea, screenplay, or concept without permission**, here's what to do:

Step 1: Gather Evidence
☑ **Find dated drafts, emails, or proof that you shared the work first.**
☑ **If you registered with WGA or the Copyright Office, get your registration details.**

Step 2: Consult an Entertainment Lawyer
☑ **They can issue a cease-and-desist letter** (often, this stops the theft before a lawsuit is necessary).
☑ **If the case is strong, you may be able to sue for damages.**

Step 3: Decide If Legal Action is Worth It

- Lawsuits **are expensive and time-consuming.**
- If the stolen work **is making millions, legal action might be necessary.**
- If it's a minor infringement, **it might be better to move on and create something new.**

Real Case Study: The "Shape of Water" Copyright Controversy

- Guillermo del Toro's *The Shape of Water* (2017) **faced accusations of being inspired by a 1969 play.**
- The lawsuit **was later dropped**, but the controversy **could have been avoided if legal protections were clearer.**

Lesson:

- **Lawsuits are complicated—registering your work early is always the best protection.**

Your Action Plan:

- If you believe your idea was stolen, **consult a lawyer before making public accusations.**
- Keep **detailed records** of who you pitch to and when.

Final Recap: How to Protect Your Intellectual Property

✓ **Register your screenplay with the WGA and U.S. Copyright Office.**
✓ **Before pitching a film or TV series, protect your idea**

legally.

✓ Use NDAs when sharing pitch decks, scripts, or treatments.

✓ Keep track of meetings, emails, and submission records.

✓ If someone steals your work, consult a lawyer and gather evidence before taking action.

Next Steps: Take Action Today

☑ If you haven't registered your screenplay, do it today (WGA or Copyright Office).

☑ If you're pitching, use NDAs to protect your concept.

☑ Keep a log of who sees your work to protect yourself legally.

4. Understanding Profit Participation & Backend Deals

What is Profit Participation?

Profit participation means **you get paid a percentage of a film's revenue instead of a flat fee.**

☑️ **"Points" (Percentage of Net or Gross Profits)** – Often given to directors, actors, and producers.
☑️ **Box Office Bonuses** – Some contracts include bonuses based on ticket sales.
☑️ **Streaming Revenue Share** – Netflix, Amazon, and others offer different payout models.

Real Case Study: How Robert Downey Jr. Made Over $75M from "Avengers"

- Downey **negotiated a backend deal** instead of a big upfront salary.
- His contract included **percentage points from box office revenue.**
- Since *Avengers: Endgame* made **$2.8 billion worldwide**, his backend cut **made him over $75M.**

Lesson:

- **A well-negotiated backend deal can make you richer than a high upfront fee.**
- **Always ask for revenue-sharing options if you believe in the project's success.**

Your Action Plan:

- **If negotiating a deal, ask for backend points instead of just an upfront fee.**
- **Make sure profit participation is based on "gross" revenue, not "net" profits** (Hollywood accounting can hide real profits).

5. Networking & Building Industry Relationships

Why Networking is the Secret to Success in Film
Hollywood isn't just about **talent**—it's about **who you know.**
☑ Most jobs in film are filled through **industry referrals, not job postings.**
☑ Getting a **good producer, DP, or actor attached** to your film often comes from networking.

Real Case Study: How Damien Chazelle Got "La La Land" Made Through Industry Connections

- Chazelle's first major film, *Whiplash*, **won Sundance and got him meetings with studios.**
- Through those meetings, he met **producers who trusted him enough to fund *La La Land*.**
- *La La Land* became a **$447M box office hit and won 6 Oscars.**

Lesson:

- **Festivals, events, and industry mixers are where deals happen.**
- **The bigger your network, the more opportunities will come your way.**

Your Action Plan:

- Attend **major film festivals and networking events** (Sundance, Cannes, TIFF).
- Join **industry organizations** like the Producers Guild of America (PGA) or Writers Guild of America (WGA).
- Connect with **other filmmakers, actors, and producers on LinkedIn & social media.**

6. Avoiding Industry Scams & Common Pitfalls

Red Flags to Watch Out For in the Film Business

▶ **Pay-to-Play Agents or Managers** – Legit agents take a commission, not upfront fees.

▶ **Producers Who Promise Funding but Want You to Pay First** – If someone says they can fund your film but **ask for money upfront**, it's a scam.

▶ **Contracts That Take Away Your Rights** – Never sign a deal that **gives away ownership of your work without proper compensation.**

🎬 **Real Case Study: How a Fake Producer Scammed Indie Filmmakers with False Promises**

- A so-called "producer" **claimed to have Netflix deals** and convinced indie filmmakers to pay him **"development fees" to pitch their projects.**
- He **never had any real industry connections**—he was just taking money.
- Filmmakers lost **tens of thousands of dollars,** and the projects never happened.

🔖 **Lesson:**

- **Legitimate producers and investors never ask you to pay them first.**
- **Always verify industry contacts before signing deals.**

Your Action Plan:

- If an offer **seems too good to be true, research the person making it.**
- Consult an **entertainment lawyer before signing anything.**

Final Recap: Mastering the Business of Filmmaking

✓ Contracts protect your rights—never sign without legal review.

✓ Backend deals can be more profitable than upfront salaries.

✓ Agents, managers, and attorneys are key to long-term success.

✓ Networking is essential—attend events, build connections, and stay active in the industry.

✓ Avoid scams and bad deals—if someone asks for

money upfront, walk away.

Next Steps: Take Action Today

☑ Review your current contracts (if any) with a legal expert.

☑ If you're ready for career representation, research agents and managers.

☑ Start networking—connect with at least five industry professionals this month.

🎬 Now that you understand the legal and business aspects, let's move to Chapter 7: Marketing & Selling Your Film!

Chapter 7:
Marketing &
Selling Your Film

You've finished your film. Now what?

No matter how good your movie is, if no one sees it, it might as well not exist. The film industry is filled with great films that never found an audience because they weren't marketed properly. On the other hand, some average films became massive hits simply because they had incredible marketing.

Marketing isn't just about selling—it's about creating excitement, building an audience, and making sure your film reaches the people who will love it.

By the end of this chapter, you will:

✅ **Understand how to market your film like a studio—
even with a small budget.**

✅ **Learn how to build an audience before your film is
released.**

✅ **Discover strategies for maximizing revenue through
online sales, theaters, and streaming.**

✅ **Gain insight into leveraging partnerships, publicity,
and film festivals for greater visibility.**

1. Why Marketing Matters as Much as Filmmaking

The Harsh Reality: A well-marketed bad movie can still
make millions. A poorly marketed great movie can
disappear overnight.

**Real Case Study: How "The Blair Witch Project" Became
a $250M Success**

- Made on a **$60K budget**, *The Blair Witch Project*
  was one of the first films to use **viral marketing.**

- The filmmakers **created fake missing-person reports online** to make it seem like the events in the film were real.
- The film made **$250 million at the box office**, proving that smart marketing can outperform big budgets.

Lesson:

- **Your film isn't just a movie—it's a product. You need to sell it.**
- **Marketing begins BEFORE your film is finished, not after.**
- **Audiences don't just buy tickets to films—they buy experiences, emotions, and stories.**

Your Action Plan:

- **Develop a marketing strategy early**—don't wait until post-production.
- **Find your audience now**—who will pay to see your film, and where do they hang out?
- **Study successful independent and studio films**—understand what worked and apply it.

2. Building an Audience Before Your Film is Released

The Biggest Mistake Filmmakers Make: They finish the film, then try to build an audience. **Start marketing from Day 1.**

How "Paranormal Activity" Built Hype Before Release

- The filmmakers **screened the film at festivals** and **encouraged audiences to demand a wider release.**
- A **viral website** allowed fans to vote on where the film should premiere.
- By the time it hit theaters, it had **massive buzz and made $193M on a $15K budget.**

How to Build an Audience Early:

☑ **Create a website & email list** – Collect emails from people interested in your film.

☑ **Start a social media presence** – Share behind-the-scenes content to engage potential fans.

☑ **Engage with niche communities** – Find forums, Facebook groups, and online spaces where your audience hangs out.

☑ **Leverage teaser campaigns** – Release short clips or sneak peeks to generate anticipation.

☑ **Network with influencers and film bloggers** – Get early support from industry voices.

Your Action Plan:

- Identify **who your audience is** and where they spend time online.
- Set up **a simple landing page and email signup** to start collecting contacts.
- Start **posting behind-the-scenes updates** on social media.
- **Plan an exclusive early screening** for targeted influencers and bloggers.

3. Using Social Media & Influencers to Market Your Film

Why Social Media Matters: You don't need a Hollywood budget to build a fanbase—you just need **smart content strategy.**

How "Deadpool" Used Social Media to Dominate Marketing

- The *Deadpool* marketing team **created viral videos, memes, and funny Twitter posts** that aligned with the film's humor.
- They **engaged directly with fans** instead of using traditional ads.

- Result? **The highest-grossing R-rated film at the time.**

How to Use Social Media Effectively for Your Film:

☑ **Post consistent, engaging content** – Share BTS footage, actor interviews, and teaser clips.

☑ **Leverage influencers** – Get YouTubers, bloggers, and social media personalities to talk about your film.

☑ **Run contests & challenges** – Encourage fans to participate by creating content related to your movie.

☑ **Go live on social media** – Interact with fans in real time to build hype.

☑ **Create behind-the-scenes documentary content** – Give audiences a peek into your process.

Your Action Plan:

- Start engaging with influencers **who align with your film's audience.**
- Plan a **content schedule** for your film's social media accounts.
- Organize **Q&A sessions, live-streams, and community discussions.**

4. Film Festivals & Press Coverage: Getting Media Attention

Why Festivals Matter: Festivals give **exposure, credibility, and access to buyers.**

Real Case Study: How "Whiplash" Used Sundance to Secure Distribution

- *Whiplash* started as a short film at **Sundance.**
- It won multiple awards, attracting **studio and distributor attention.**
- Became a **feature film, grossing $49M worldwide and winning 3 Oscars.**

How to Use Festivals to Market Your Film:

☑ **Target the right festivals** – Research which festivals match your film's genre.

☑ **Network aggressively** – Meet distributors, journalists, and influencers at events.

☑ **Submit to film blogs & press** – Get reviews and features to build credibility.

Your Action Plan:

- Make a list of **top film festivals** that fit your film's niche.
- Reach out to **film journalists and critics** to cover your festival screenings.
- Submit your film to **multiple festivals** for maximum exposure.

Final Recap: How to Market & Sell Your Film

✔ **Start marketing early—don't wait until after the film is finished.**

✔ **Use social media, press, and influencers to build awareness.**

✔ **Film festivals can open doors to buyers and media exposure.**

✔ **Choose the right distribution path to maximize revenue.**

Next Steps: Take Action Today

☑ **Create a marketing plan for your film NOW.**

☑ Engage with influencers, festivals, and press before release.

☑ Decide if you'll go with traditional distribution or self-distribution.

Chapter 8:
Building a Sustainable Career in the Film Industry

Making one film is an achievement. Building a career in film is a lifelong journey.

Many filmmakers create one movie and then struggle to find their next opportunity. The key to longevity in this industry is not just talent—it's strategy, adaptability, and knowing how to position yourself for long-term success.

If you want to transition from making one film to making a living as a filmmaker, this chapter will give you a clear, practical roadmap.

By the end of this chapter, you will:

✅ **Understand how to establish yourself in the film industry**

✅ **Learn how to create long-term opportunities and financial stability**

✅ **Discover strategies for networking, branding, and career growth**

✅ **Know how to transition from one film to the next while maintaining momentum**

1. The Mindset of a Career Filmmaker

Filmmaking is a Business, Not Just an Art

Many filmmakers focus so much on creativity that they **forget to plan for longevity.** The reality is:

- You need **consistent income** to sustain a career.
- You must **build relationships** to stay relevant.
- You should always be working on **your next project.**

Real Case Study: How Christopher Nolan Built a Lasting Career

- Nolan **started with low-budget indie films** (*Following*, *Memento*).
- He used his **first successes to get bigger budgets** (*Batman Begins, Inception*).
- He consistently **delivered high-quality films**, ensuring **studios kept investing in him.**

Lesson:

- **Think long-term.** Your first film is just the beginning.
- **Every project should build momentum for the next one.**

Your Action Plan:

- Start **developing your next project** while finishing your current one.
- Focus on **networking with industry professionals** who can open doors for future work.

2. How to Establish Yourself in the Film Industry

Ways to Get Noticed & Stay Relevant:
☑ **Film Festivals & Awards** – Build credibility and industry

buzz. ✅ **Online Presence & Social Media** – Showcase your work and connect with filmmakers. ✅ **Industry Networking Events** – Meet key decision-makers face-to-face. ✅**Collaborations with Other Filmmakers** – Gain experience and exposure. ✅ **Consistent Content Creation** – Don't just make one film—keep producing work.

Real Case Study: How Ava DuVernay Went from Indie Filmmaker to Hollywood Powerhouse

- DuVernay started with **self-funded indie films.**
- She used **film festivals to build recognition** (*Middle of Nowhere* won at Sundance).
- She leveraged her success to **secure major studio deals** (*Selma, A Wrinkle in Time*).

Lesson:

- **Film festivals, networking, and consistent work all contribute to longevity.**
- **Your career is a marathon, not a sprint.**

Your Action Plan:

- Submit your work to **festivals that match your genre.**
- Connect with **producers, agents, and distributors** at industry events.
- **Keep making films**—even if they're short films or web projects.

3. Networking & Relationship-Building for Long-Term Success

Why Networking is Essential:
In the film industry, **who you know is just as important as what you know.** Many film deals happen through relationships, not formal applications.

Real Case Study: How Ryan Coogler Landed "Black Panther" Through Industry Connections

- Coogler made a **low-budget indie film (*Fruitvale Station*) that won Sundance.**
- Through festival networking, he met **Hollywood executives who backed *Creed*.**
- After proving himself, **Marvel hired him to direct *Black Panther*.**

Where to Network in the Film Industry: ☑ **Film Festivals (Sundance, Cannes, TIFF, SXSW, etc.)** ☑ **Industry Conferences (Produced By Conference, NAB, AFM, etc.)** ☑ **Social Media & LinkedIn (Follow industry leaders and engage in discussions)** ☑ **Local Filmmaker Meetups & Groups** ☑ **Joining Industry Organizations (PGA, WGA, DGA, etc.)**

Your Action Plan:

- Attend at least **one major film festival per year.**
- Build **genuine relationships with industry professionals.**
- Connect with **filmmakers and executives on LinkedIn.**

4. Securing Financial Stability as a Filmmaker

How to Keep Income Flowing Between Projects: ☑ **Freelance in Film & TV Production** – Work as a DP, editor, or producer on other projects. ☑ **Film Grants & Fellowships** – Apply for funding programs that support filmmakers. ☑ **Teaching or Consulting** – Offer expertise to new filmmakers. ☑ **Investing in Yourself** – Learn about film financing and business strategies. ☑ **Crowdfunding & Patron Support** – Platforms like Patreon can provide steady income.

Real Case Study: How Kevin Smith Used Direct-to-Fan Sales to Build a Business

- After *Clerks*, Smith realized **he didn't need Hollywood to make money.**

- He built a **direct relationship with fans** through podcasts, merchandise, and special screenings.
- He now **self-finances films and sells them directly to his audience.**

Lesson:

- **Find multiple revenue streams so you're not relying on one film to succeed.**
- **Your brand as a filmmaker can generate income beyond just making movies.**

Your Action Plan:

- Diversify your income **through multiple creative ventures.**
- Learn about **film business models and financing.**

Final Recap: How to Build a Long-Term Career in Film

✓ Think long-term—one film is just the beginning of your career. ✓ Establish yourself through festivals, networking, and consistent work. ✓ Build strong industry relationships—who you know matters. ✓ Create multiple income streams to stay financially stable. ✓ Leverage indie success to transition into bigger projects.

Next Steps: Take Action Today

☑ Develop a long-term career plan—where do you want to be in 5 years? ☑ Attend networking events or film festivals to grow your connections. ☑ Diversify your income to sustain your career between projects. ☑ Start preparing your next film while promoting your current one.

Now that you have a career roadmap, it's time to put your knowledge into action!

Chapter 9:
Final Steps to Achieving Success in the Film Industry

Filmmaking is a journey, not a single destination. Success in the film industry is not just about making one great movie—it's about sustaining a career, building meaningful relationships, and continuously adapting to the ever-changing landscape of entertainment.

This chapter will help you solidify your path forward, ensuring that you don't just make a film, but that you build a lasting career in film.

By the end of this chapter, you will:
☑ **Understand how to maintain momentum after completing your film.**
☑ **Learn how to leverage your success for bigger opportunities.**

☑ Master strategies for career longevity and brand-building.

☑ Develop a clear next-step plan to keep progressing.

1. How to Maintain Momentum After Your Film is Released

Why Many Filmmakers Struggle After Their First Film

- Many independent filmmakers put everything into making one film and then don't know what to do next.
- Without a plan to keep the momentum going, filmmakers often disappear from the industry after their first project.

Real Case Study: How Barry Jenkins Leveraged "Moonlight" for Career Longevity

- After winning the Oscar for *Moonlight*, Jenkins did not just sit back and wait for offers.
- He immediately started working on *If Beale Street Could Talk* and took on TV projects.
- He positioned himself as an in-demand director and storyteller.

Real Case Study: How Kevin Smith Turned Independent

Success into a Career

- After *Clerks*, Kevin Smith **built a direct relationship with his audience** via podcasts, merchandise, and touring live shows.
- This allowed him to keep making films without relying on studios.
- He created a sustainable **indie ecosystem** that has kept his career alive for decades.

Lesson:

- **Your film's success is only as strong as what you do next.**
- **Keep pitching new ideas, networking, and securing your next project before the hype dies down.**
- **Leverage different revenue streams (merch, speaking engagements, online courses) to maintain financial stability between films.**

Your Action Plan:

- **Announce your next project immediately after your film is released** to keep industry interest high.
- **Engage with your audience regularly**—use YouTube, Patreon, or social media to stay connected.

- **Explore multiple revenue opportunities**—merchandising, online courses, crowdfunding for future projects.
- **Seek collaborations**—team up with fellow filmmakers on upcoming projects to stay active.

2. Leveraging Your Film's Success for Bigger Opportunities

How to Use Your First Film as a Springboard

- Whether your film wins awards or gets critical acclaim, it should serve as your **calling card** for bigger projects.
- Filmmakers who leverage their early success wisely land bigger budgets, studio deals, and higher-profile collaborators.

Real Case Study: How Damien Chazelle Used "Whiplash" to Land "La La Land"

- Chazelle's indie success with *Whiplash* proved his directing talent.
- He used that success to pitch *La La Land* to studios, leading to a $30M budget and six Academy Awards.

Real Case Study: How Greta Gerwig Transitioned from Indie Darling to Studio Director

- Gerwig started with micro-budget indie films and critical darlings like *Lady Bird*.
- Her proven talent secured her *Little Women* and later *Barbie*, which became a billion-dollar hit.
- She demonstrated the ability to transition from indie filmmaking to large-scale productions.

Lesson:

- **A great first film can be your launchpad—but only if you actively use it to move forward.**
- **Be strategic about what your next project is— capitalize on the themes, success, and style that made your first film work.**

Your Action Plan:

- **Develop a strategy** for how you will use your film's momentum to pitch new projects.
- **Reach out to studios, agents, and producers** while your film is still fresh in the industry's mind.
- **Keep building your portfolio**—whether it's another feature film, TV, or branded content.

3. Building Your Brand as a Filmmaker

Why Branding Matters in Film

- A successful career in film isn't just about making good movies—it's about making sure people know **who you are** and what you stand for.
- Filmmakers with strong personal brands (Quentin Tarantino, Jordan Peele, Greta Gerwig) attract more opportunities.

Real Case Study: How Jordan Peele Built a Recognizable Brand

- After *Get Out*, Peele established himself as a **master of intelligent horror.**
- His unique storytelling style made him one of Hollywood's most sought-after directors.

Lesson:

- **Define what makes you unique as a filmmaker.**
- **Your brand should be consistent across interviews, social media, and new projects.**

Your Action Plan:

- Establish **your niche**—what kind of films do you want to be known for?
- Build an **authentic online presence** that showcases your work and ideas.
- Be active in **film communities, panels, and discussions** to solidify your reputation.

Final Recap: Your Roadmap to Film Industry Success

✓ **Momentum is everything—have your next project lined up before your first one is finished.** ✓ **Leverage your film's success to land bigger projects and new opportunities.** ✓ **Your brand as a filmmaker matters—define your niche and own it.** ✓ **Plan for the long-term—think beyond one film to create a sustainable career.** ✓ **Use multiple income streams to sustain yourself between projects.**

Next Steps: Your Personalized Action Plan

☑ **Set clear career goals for the next 5 years.**

☑ Establish an industry network that supports your growth.

☑ Start developing your next film while promoting your current one.

☑ Use marketing, branding, and networking to keep yourself visible in the industry.

☑ Diversify your income sources to sustain yourself between films.

This is just the beginning—your filmmaking journey doesn't stop here. Keep pushing forward, learning, and growing. The industry belongs to those who refuse to give up.

Chapter 10:
The Filmmaker's Playbook – Your Path Forward

Filmmaking is a journey, not a single destination. Success in the film industry is not just about making one great movie—it's about sustaining a career, building meaningful relationships, and continuously adapting to the ever-changing landscape of entertainment.

This chapter will help you solidify your path forward, ensuring that you don't just make a film, but that you build a lasting career in film.

By the end of this chapter, you will:

☑ **Understand how to maintain momentum after completing your film**

☑ **Learn how to leverage your success for bigger opportunities**

☑ **Master strategies for career longevity and brand-building**
☑ **Develop a clear next-step plan to keep progressing**

1. The Filmmaker's Mindset: Turning Knowledge into Action

Why Some Filmmakers Succeed While Others Struggle

- The difference between those who **make it** in the film industry and those who **don't** isn't just talent—it's persistence, adaptability, and strategy.
- Filmmakers who keep moving forward despite setbacks ultimately find success.

Real Case Study: How Robert Rodriguez Refused to Give Up

- Rodriguez **made *El Mariachi* for just $7,000**, which led to Hollywood opportunities.
- He didn't stop there—he kept making films and building a sustainable career.
- He later became one of the most successful independent filmmakers by **leveraging creative financing and direct distribution.**

Lesson:

- **You don't need permission from Hollywood to succeed.**
- **Use what you've learned in this book and start NOW.**

Your Action Plan:

- **Decide TODAY what your next step will be.**
- Whether it's writing a new script, applying to a festival, or pitching your next project, **take immediate action.**

2. Overcoming the Fear of Failure: Every Filmmaker Faces Setbacks

Why Fear Holds Filmmakers Back

- Many talented filmmakers never achieve success because they are **afraid to fail**.
- Every great filmmaker has had **films rejected, projects scrapped, and funding fall through**.

Real Case Study: How Kathryn Bigelow Proved Critics Wrong

- Bigelow was told female directors wouldn't succeed in action films.
- She **pushed forward and became the first woman to win the Academy Award for Best Director** (*The Hurt Locker*).

Lesson:

- **Failure is just another step toward success.**
- **You only truly fail when you stop trying.**

Your Action Plan:

- Identify **one fear that is holding you back** and **face it head-on.**
- Accept that rejection and setbacks are part of the process.

3. Building a Sustainable Career: Your 5-Year Roadmap

Where Will You Be in 5 Years?

- The best filmmakers don't just **think about their next film—they think about the next five films.**

- Success doesn't happen overnight, but **with a long-term plan, you will keep progressing.**

Your 5-Year Filmmaking Roadmap:

☑ **Year 1:** Develop and market a project (short film, feature, or series).

☑ **Year 2:** Expand your industry network through festivals, online presence, and collaborations.

☑ **Year 3:** Secure distribution or funding for your next big project.

☑ **Year 4:** Leverage your success to attract bigger budgets and partners.

☑ **Year 5:** Become a recognized filmmaker in your genre/niche.

Lesson:

- **Filmmaking is a long game—plan ahead, stay focused, and keep building.**

Your Action Plan:

- Write down a **5-year plan** for your filmmaking career.
- Break it down into **smaller goals** that can be achieved each year.

4. Final Words: You Have Everything You Need—Now Go Create!

You've Learned the Blueprint—Now It's Time to Execute

- Every chapter in this book has given you **industry knowledge, case studies, and actionable strategies**.
- **But knowledge alone isn't enough.** The only way to succeed is to **take action.**

Real Case Study: How Steven Spielberg Created His Own Opportunities

- Spielberg **snuck onto Universal's lot as a teenager**, pretending to be an employee.
- He **created his own short film**, which eventually got him noticed by the studio.
- Instead of waiting for an opportunity, **he made his own.**

Lesson:

- **No one is going to hand you success—you have to take it.**
- **Start today. Write. Shoot. Edit. Pitch. Network.**

Your Final Action Plan:

☑ Choose your next film project and set a deadline to complete it.

☑ Make a daily habit of writing, filming, networking, or studying the craft.

☑ Never stop learning, never stop creating, and never stop pushing forward.

Closing Thought:
Your Filmmaking Journey Starts Now

The greatest filmmakers weren't necessarily the most talented or well-connected—they were the ones who refused to quit.

☑ Take what you've learned in this book and apply it immediately.

☑ Your future in film is in your hands—go make it happen.

ACKNOWLEDGEMENTS

No journey is ever taken alone, and this book is no exception. It is the culmination of years of experience, insight, and inspiration drawn from the incredible individuals who have shaped my path in the film industry.

First and foremost, I want to express my deepest gratitude to those who have mentored, challenged, and encouraged me throughout my career. Your wisdom and generosity have been invaluable, and your belief in my vision has fueled my passion for storytelling.

To my colleagues, collaborators and the many talented professionals I've had the privilege of working alongside—thank you for your creativity, dedication, and relentless pursuit of excellence. Your work continues to inspire me, and I am honored to have shared projects with such remarkable minds.

To my friends and family, your unwavering support, patience, and encouragement have been my foundation. Thank you for believing in me even when the path was uncertain. Your love and understanding have been my greatest source of strength.

And to you, the reader—whether you are an aspiring filmmaker, an industry veteran, or someone simply curious about the world of film—thank you for allowing me to share my insights with you. It is my hope that this book empowers you, enlightens you, and serves as a valuable guide on your own creative journey.

This book is not just mine—it belongs to everyone who has played a role in my journey. To all of you, I am forever grateful.

– Milo Schwartz

ABOUT THE AUTHOR

Milo Schwartz is a seasoned film executive and storyteller with **35 years of experience** in the film, television and commercial production industries. His work has been showcased on major platforms such as **HBO, CBS, SHOWTIME, HULU, The CW Network, TV ONE and BET**, captivating audiences with authentic narratives and visually compelling content across diverse genres. Beyond entertainment, Milo's creative expertise has extended to collaborations with global brands like **Ford Motor Company, Ace Hardware, NIKE, AT&T and Volkswagen**, where he has skillfully crafted engaging stories that resonate across generations. Known for his meticulous attention to detail and innovative approach to storytelling, Milo continues to push the boundaries of content creation, blending artistic vision with strategic insight to leave a lasting impact in both the entertainment and corporate worlds.

www.filmbusiness101.com